Pocket
ACTIVITY
FUN and GAMES

PIRATES

Join this merry pirate crew.
They need a pirate just like YOU!
So turn the page and take a look –
they're waiting for you in this book!

What's inside this book?

Stickers

Use the stickers on the sticker scenes, puzzle pages, and anywhere else you want to!

Puzzle fun

Find your way through a shark-infested maze, follow the stars at night, spot the differences, and other tough tests!

Stories and pictures

There are plenty of things for pirates to write, draw, and paint, so why not get going now!

Games

Read a treasure map on page 60 and play an exciting pirate wars game on page 78.

This is a Carlton book

Text, design and illustrations copyright © 2013 Carlton Books Limited

Published in 2013 by Carlton Books Ltd
An imprint of the Carlton Publishing Group
20 Mortimer Street, London, W1T 3JW

A catalogue record for this book is available from the British Library.

ISBN: 978-1-78312-000-0

Printed in Heshan, China

Author: Andrea Pinnington

Calling all pirates!

Have you got what it takes to be a PIRATE? Answer the questions below to find out!

☠ Do you dream of finding buried treasure?

☠ Are you tough, mean, clever, and fearless? Yes

☠ Are any of your teeth missing? NO

☠ Do you long to sail the seas? Yes

If you've answered yes to most of the above, then this is the perfect book for you!

The world of pirates

Do you want to become a TOP PIRATE? Simply complete the easy steps below...

← Draw yourself as a pirate here. Will you be a mean, terrifying, dirty or friendly pirate?

Now choose your ship (check the one you want)

☐ Chinese junk

☐ schooner

☐ galleon

☐ Greek galley

What job will you do on board?
(check the right box)

☑ captain
(the boss
of the ship)

☐ surgeon
(looks after
injured pirates)

☑ first mate
(hands out
food and
treasure)

☑ stowaway
(sneaks on board
ship without
anyone seeing)

☑ gunner
(fires the
cannons)

☑ cabin boy
(does all the
worst jobs)

"Be prepared" is a
popular pirate motto.
Make your first
treasure map NOW so
that you are ready to
hide any treasure you
come across.

How to draw a pirate

First, draw a circle for the head with a line going across the middle of it. Then draw a square body.

Good start!

Copy each step-by-step drawing into the boxes below.

Draw two lines between the square and the circle for the neck. Add two arms and some pants.

Getting there!

Put a circle and triangle next to his head to make a bandana. Now give your pirate hands and boots.

Almost done!

Finally, this pirate needs eyes, a mouth, a dagger, an eye patch, a belt, and spots on his bandana.

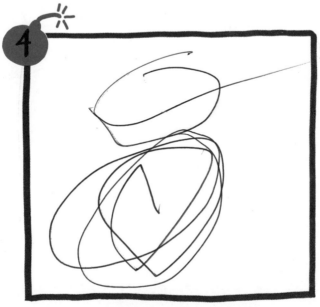

Great work!

9

Pirate paper
and what to do with it!

1 Cut out the CLOTHES on the back of your pirate paper. Stick them where they belong (see page 15) for another pirate job well done!

2 Make some EDIBLE BOATS using your pirate paper for sails! Ask a grown-up to cut an orange into quarters, then use a cocktail stick for a mast to hold your sails in place.

3 Cut out one of the spectacular pirate paper designs. Roll it up to form a tube and tape the end in place. Now you have your very own TELESCOPE.

pirate hat

vest

Cut out these shapes, then find out where they belong.

pirate hat

boy underwear

boy underwear

pirate hat

vest

T-shirt

11

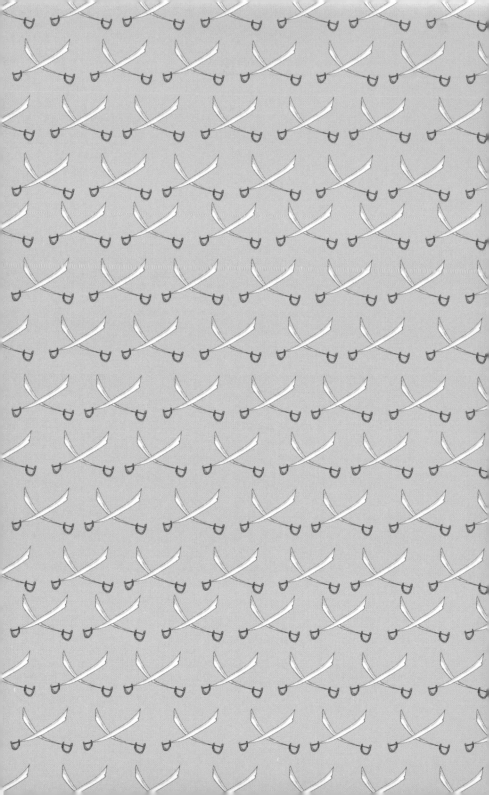

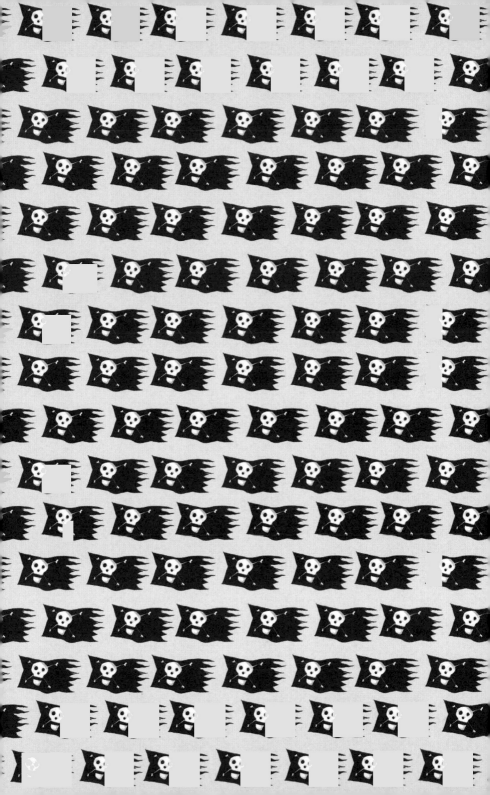

neckerchief

pants

Cut out these shapes, then find out where they belong.

pirate hat

boy underwear

vest

T-shirt

cat jacket

boy underwear

bandana

14

Pirates on parade

Stick the paper clothes on these rascals and help them to get their ship ready to sail.

Annual pirate washing day Bring out your undies now!

Complete the clothesline.

Hang some pirate clothes here.

16

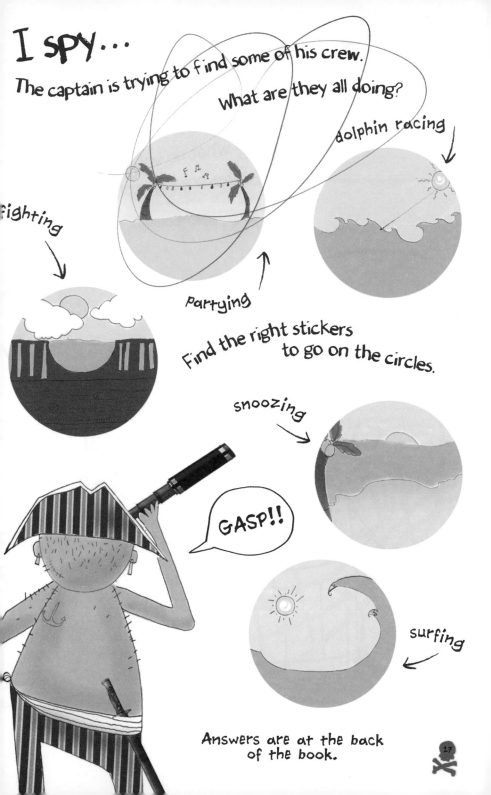

Pirate cookies

Lots of pirates LOVE to cook.

Here's one of their secret recipes.

Makes about 15 cookies –
enough for 6 hungry pirates

You will need

- ★ 6 oz (175 g) plain flour
- ★ 4 oz (100 g) butter
- ★ 2 oz (50 g) caster sugar
- ★ 7 oz (200 g) icing sugar
- ★ 2–3 tablespoons of water
- ★ food coloring
- ★ water

How to make the cookies

★ Pre-heat oven to 300°F (150°C).

★ Line a baking tray with greaseproof paper.

★ Mix the butter and sugar together until they are light and fluffy.

★ Stir in the flour and mix together until it forms a ball (add a bit of water if needed).

★ Roll out the dough on a lightly floured surface until it is about as thick as your little finger.

★ Cut out the dough using an upside-down glass, mug, or cookie cutter if you have one.

★ Put the cookies on the baking tray and bake for 10-15 minutes or until golden brown.

★ Pop the cookies onto a wire rack to cool before decorating.

How to make the icing

★ Sift the icing sugar into a large bowl.

★ Stir in the water until you have a smooth paste.

★ Divide the icing up if you want to make different colors.

★ Add a few drops of coloring to each bit of icing and use to decorate your pirate cookies.

Bearded buccaneers

Make this crew of pirates super hairy by drawing some beards and mustaches.

Barry the Bearded
People often wonder whether animals live inside Barry's MASSIVE beard!

Captain Ugly
This horrible villain's nostrils and ears are the hairiest on the seven seas!

Sly the Stubbly
So hairy is Sly, he has to
shave FOUR times a day!

Mustaches Marv
Quite the dandy, Marv
spends a long time
grooming his mega
mustache.

Avoid these pirates
at all costs...

Selina the Surprisingly Hairy
Most female pirates are hairy.
Selina arranges her beard into
interesting shapes.

Land ahoy!

Use your stickers and colored pencils here.

Pirate things to color in

coins

dagger

pirate boot

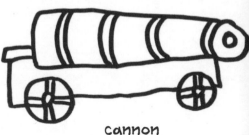

cannon

hook

treasure chest

ship's wheel

tropical island

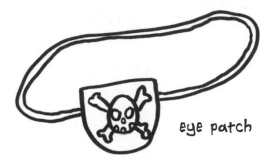

eye patch

ship

drinks

Pirate school

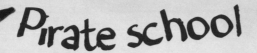

Some young pirates are learning to read maps. Can you help them work out what objects can be found at these points on the treasure map?

$\longrightarrow$

TOP TIP:
Put one finger on the letter and one finger on the number and move your fingers in a straight line down and across until your fingers meet.

B3

F1

A5

E3

H8

28

Answers are at the back of the book.

Pretty Pollies

Give these parrots some color.

A day in the life

Draw lines to connect the pictures with the pirate activities. Then write in the missing words.

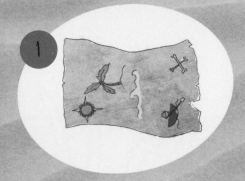

1

a sailing the seven _ _ _ _

2

b hobbling on one _ _ _

3

c _ _ _ _-reading

d finding

_ _ _ _ _

4

5

e stowing

_ _ _ _ _

f _ _ _ _ fighting

6

Answers are at the back of the book.

Ship's stores

stinky cheese

soup   more soup

...ll the shelves with food,
ready for a long sea voyage.

maggoty meat

Spot the difference

Can you spot 10 differences between these pirate pictures?

1 2 3 4 5

Check off the differences as you find each one.

6 7 8 9 10

Answers are at the back of the book.

Top hats

Add some bows and buckles to these stylish hats, then color them in.

39

What can they see?

land ahoy?

Draw in the objects that you think these pirates can see in the distance.

Trapped on a desert island, the lonely pirate looks
out to sea. Suddenly, there appears...

Colorful characters

Here are a few of the most terrible pirates that have ever lived. Read about their fearsome ways and color in their pictures.

Sir Henry Morgan

This fancy dresser made many successful raids on passing ships. He was said to be very cruel and was also known as The Buccaneer King.

Blackbeard

Blackbeard was one of the most famous pirates of all. Tall, bearded, dark, and terrifying, he would make himself even scarier by putting lighted matches under his hat!

Ching Shih

Ching Shih was one of the fiercest pirates that ever lived. Her punishments were terrible and she destroyed over 60 Chinese naval ships.

Captain Kidd

William Kidd started out as a pirate hunter but decided to become a pirate himself! Sadly, he was killed, but it is said that he hid his bounty, which has not yet been discovered...

Black Bart

This well-dressed fellow was captured by pirates as a young man. You might think this made him unhappy, but no! He became one of the most successful pirates ever.

Monsters of the deep
Color in and name these fearsome undersea creatures!

Oscar

5 reasons why I am a real pirate

1 I love... (for example, treasure)
_____

2 I hate...
_____

3 I always...
_____

4 I am good at...
_____

5 I wear...
_____

Signed by:
_____

WANTED

Complete this picture of the world's most wanted pirate. Use the description below or make up your own pirate face.

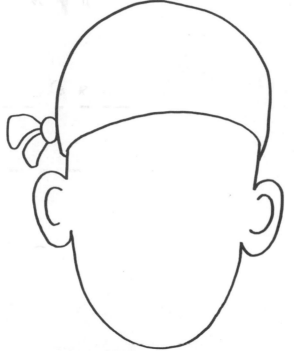

PIRATE NAME: Captain Cutlass
REAL NAME: Edward Broadside
AGE: 24

IDENTIFYING MARKS: scar on left cheek, hooked nose, curly black hair, stubbly beard, blue eyes, front tooth missing

REWARD: 300,000,000 doubloons

Underwater world

Color in this underwater scene using all the colors of the ocean!

Smugglers' rest

Follow the lines to find out where
the smugglers will stash their booty.

ead Man's Cave

Shingles Bay

Cuthbert's Creek

Answer is at the back of the book.

Shipwrecked!

There are 10 differences between these pirate pictures. Can you spot them all?

Answers are at the back of the book.

The ghost ship

Write your own pirate story.

Once upon a time
_____

_____

_____

Suddenly, there appeared
_____

_____

_____

Out of the mist,
_____

_____

_____

_____

_____

The **E**nd

(draw and name a picture here)

Those who saw the ghost ship
were never heard of again.

Pirate Pete's parrot

Copy Pirate Pete's parrot into the bird cage below.
Try drawing one square at a time.

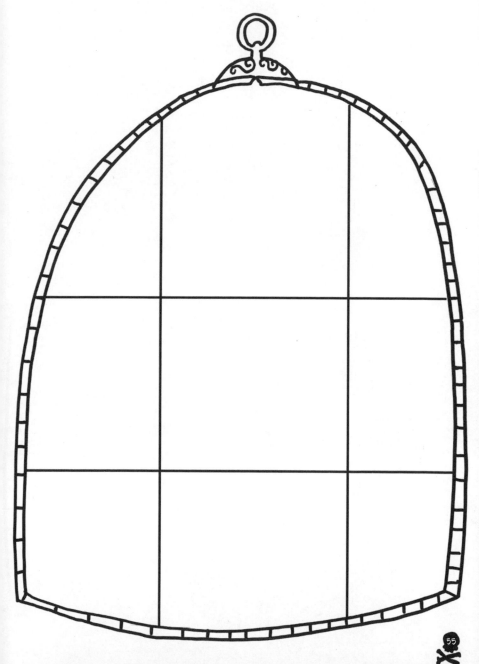

Follow the stars

Pirates use groups of stars in the sky
to work out which way to go.
Connect the dots to help the pirates find their way.

7

2 3 4

1   6

5

**Ursa Major
(the big dipper)**

1

4 3 2

12

11   5

10   **Scorpio
(the scorpion)**

6

9   8   7

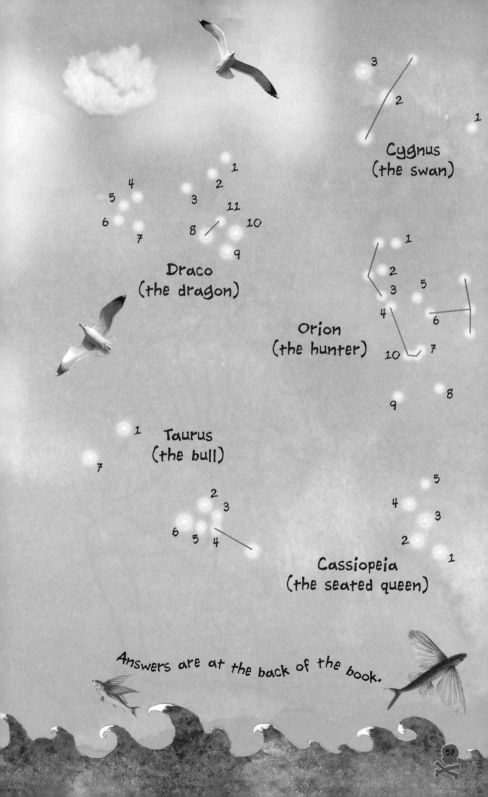

Cygnus
(the swan)

3
2
1

Draco
(the dragon)

1
2
4
3
5
6
11
7
8
10
9

Orion
(the hunter)

1
2
3
5
4
6
10
7
9
8

Taurus
(the bull)

1
7
2
3
6 5 4

Cassiopeia
(the seated queen)

5
4
3
2
1

Answers are at the back of the book.

57

North, south, east, or west?

Learn how to read a treasure map!

Top pirates need to know how to read a compass. Here's an easy way to remember the compass points, starting at north and going around in a circle:

NEVER	EAT	SOGGY	WAFFLES
(north)	(east)	(south)	(west)

Now, test yourself using the questions below...

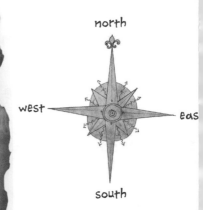

1. What lies NORTH of the lighthouse?

....

2. What is EAST from the swordfish?

....

3. What is SOUTH of the treasure map?

....

Answers are at the back of the book.

You will need
this to steer
your ship.

The pirate
sign of death.

Pirate
sticker
quiz

Which stickers
belong here?

A pirate without
one of these would
look a bit silly.

Sits on your
shoulder and makes
a lot of noise.

Also called "pieces
of eight."

What every pirate
would like to find.

Answers are at the back of the book.

The Jolly Roger

A pirate flag is called a Jolly Roger. Pirates fly them to frighten other ships. Color in these real Jolly Rogers, then make up one of your own.

The most famous JOLLY ROGER is the skull and crossbones. This one is wearing a bandana!

This skull is facing sideways. Whichever way the skull faces, it always means DEATH!

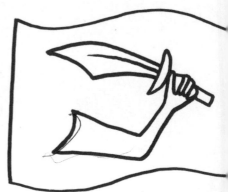

Pirates use SWORDS and DAGGERS to show they are powerful. Power to the pirates!

This flag belonged to pirate THOMAS TEW. He was killed by a sword like this one.

Design your own pirate flag

Now draw and color in your own Jolly Roger!

Ripping yarns

Make up your own pirate story using these pictures.

_____

_____

_____

_____   _____

Draw in the ending to your story.

...and he/she/they lived happily ever after!

(circle the right word)

Odd one out

Look sharp! Can you find the odd one out among these ship's cooks?

Answer is at the back of the book.

Squares for Pirate doodles

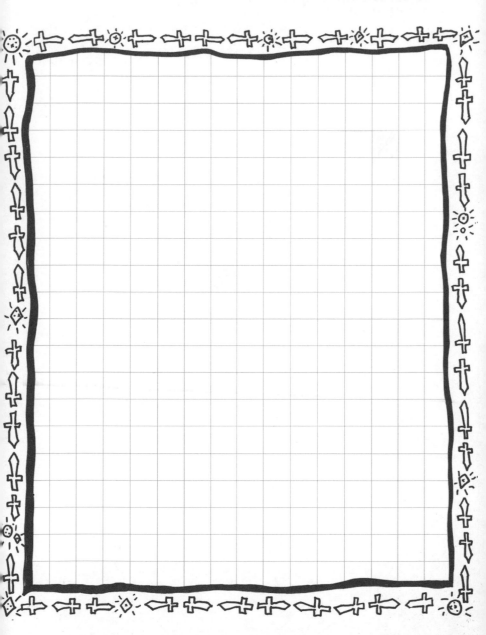

Treasure hunt

Answer is at the back of the book.

These pirates are trying to reach the treasure chest! Help them find the safe route through the shark-infested waters...

Pirate booty

Which pirate has the most treasure?

Bob

Pete

Cindy

Each piece of treasure is worth a different amount. Using the key below, add up each pirate's treasure. Then write down the name of the richest one.

	4
	2
	3

Pirate Moneybags is:
_____

Answer is at the back of the book.

Parachuting Pirates

Design two pretty parachutes for these plucky pirates.

What are the pirates saying?

Eye, eye, captain

Draw a pirate face to go with this eye patch.

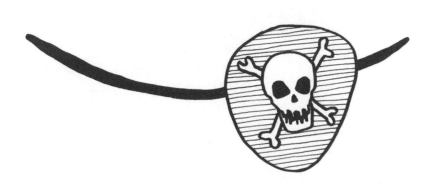

It's a pirate's life...

Grab some colored pencils and make this picture shipshape.

This ship needs a → captain.

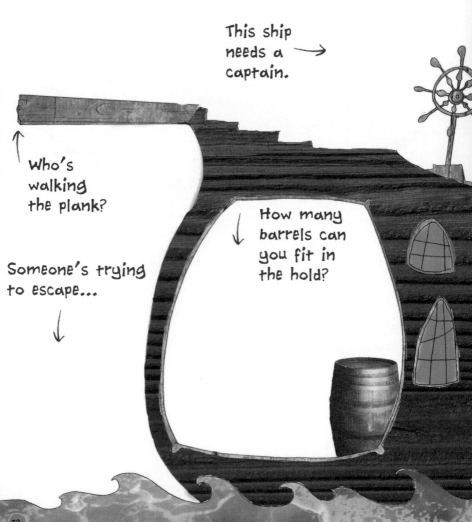

Who's walking the plank?

How many barrels can you fit in the hold?

Someone's trying to escape...

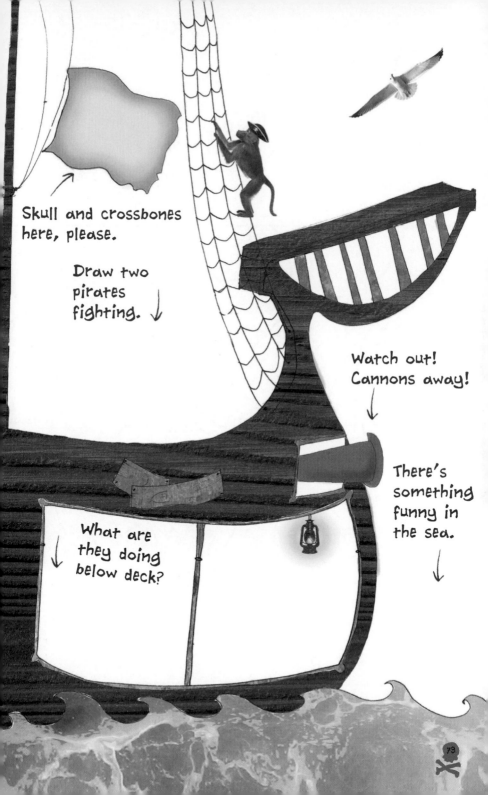

Setting sail

Color in the shapes with a dot to reveal something you need to sail a pirate ship.

74

Answer is at the back of the book.

Message in a bottle

A bottle with a secret message has washed up on shore. But what secrets does it reveal? Write a message below.

To:..

Message:......................................

....

....

....

From:..

The Pirate Times

READ ALL ABOUT THE LATEST PIRATE ADVENTURES AND DRAW SOME PICTURES TO GO WITH THEM

GUESS WHO'S WALKING THE PLANK?

After a big battle yesterday, a number of soldiers have been captured. The pirate captain, Scarface, is making them walk the plank this afternoon. If you would like to watch, please go to the dock at 3 pm in order to get a good seat. Refreshments available.

Nervous soldiers getting ready to walk the plank

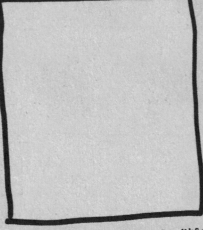

Strange sea creature reported

TERROR ON THE HIGH SEAS!

The man who walked out of the sea has finally spoken about his terrifying ordeal. He claims that a sea monster crushed his ship in its tentacles. He jumped free and swam for days before being washed up here.

Quick draw

Yo, ho, ho! Complete the pirate captain's face, then color it in.

Pirate wars

Who will be first to find the treasure?

1 CUT out the maps along the dotted lines. Keep one and give the other to another pirate.

2 HIDE 6 lots of treasure on your map, marked with an X. Don't let anyone see!

3 Take turns to CALL OUT a square (for example, E4). The pirate who is not calling shouts out FOUND or MISSED. The caller then marks F for found or M for missed in the right square.

4 The first pirate to find all the other pirate's treasure is THE WINNER!

5 Turn your paper over to play PIRATE WARS again! Make sure you both use the same map each time.

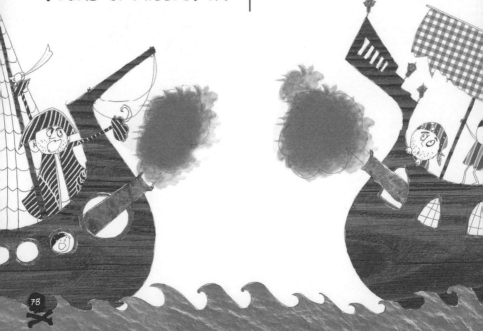

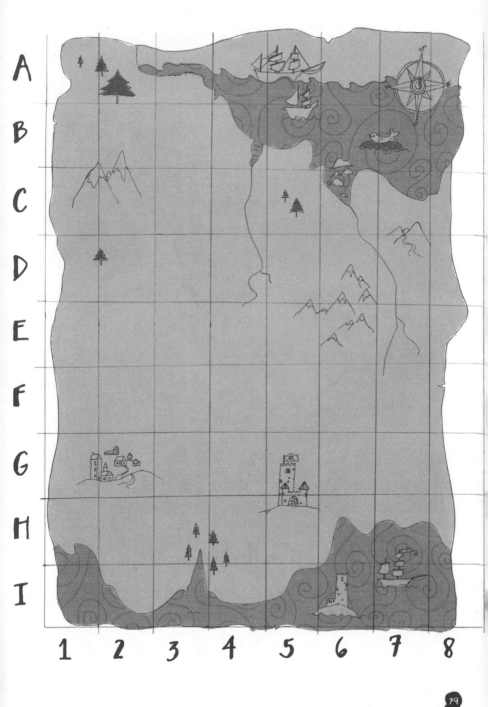

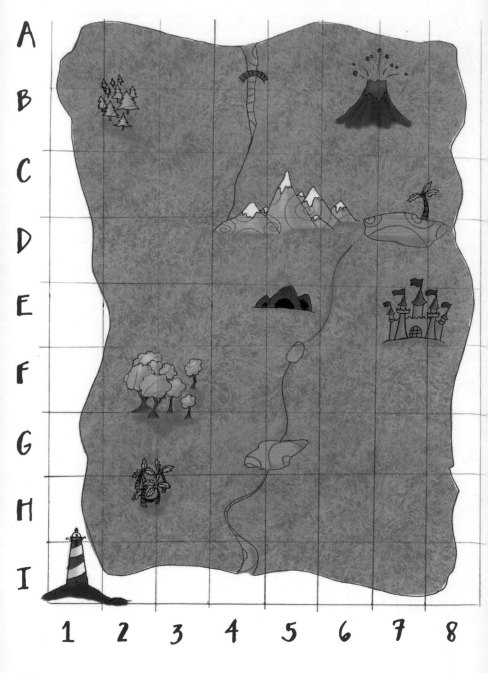

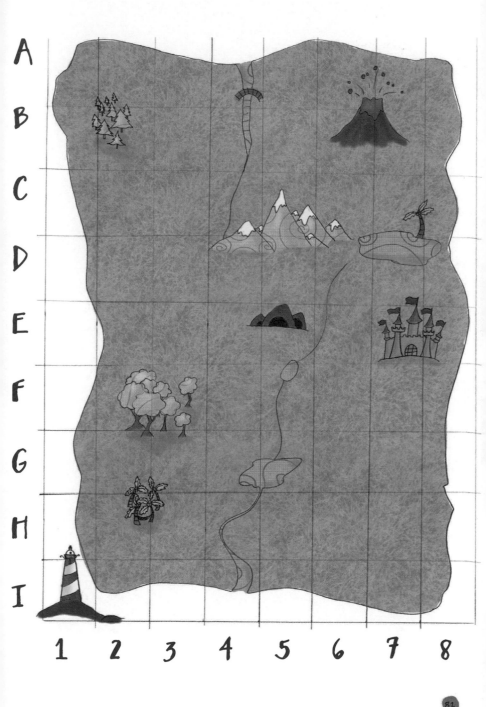

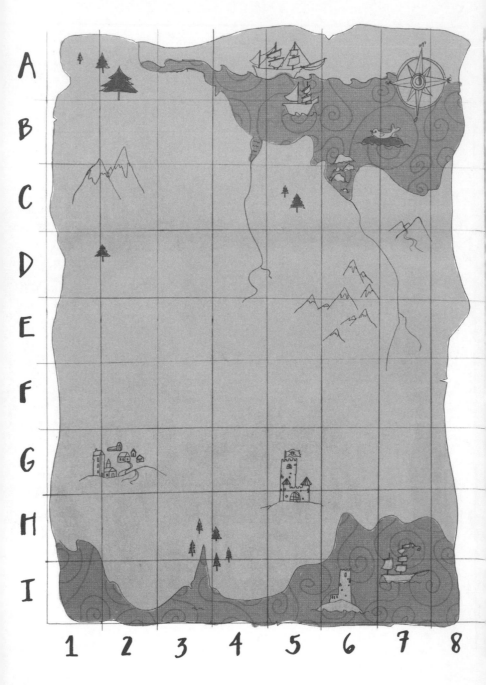

A
B
C
D
E
F
G
H
I

1 2 3 4 5 6 7 8

Pirate stickers

and what to do with them!

1 You can use your stickers on the fold-out pirate scene and on the sticker quiz pages. Plus, look out for the pages where you can also use them: 17, 24, 34, 58, 63, 72, 76.

2 Use the stickers to DECORATE your room, notebooks, suitcases, and boxes. Always ask a grown-up first.

3 For your own PIRATE POST, use the stickers to decorate cards, letters, or even party invitations.

Pirate pair

a

b

c

Spot the two pirate ships that are exactly the same.

d

e

f

Answer is at the back
of the book.

Double the doubloons

Copy the coins into grid below to earn yourself twice as much treasure!

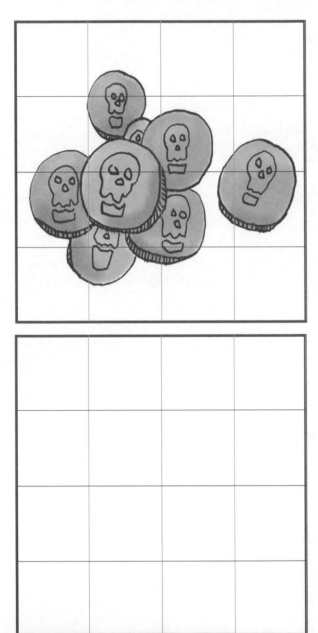

All at sea

Color in this pirate picture.

How many pirates can you find?

Answer is at the back of the book.

Quick quiz

Check the boxes in this fun quiz to see whether you'd make a perfect pirate!

1

A pirate captain asks you to join his crew. What do you say?

A No thanks, you'd miss your home too much.

B Sure, as long as you're back by dawn.

C Aye, aye, cap'n! You love traveling and exploring new places.

2

Dinner tonight is vegetable soup followed by fruit salad. Would you eat it?

A Sounds delicious! What a healthy meal.

B You'd prefer some ship's biscuits.

C Bleurgh! You hate all fruit and veggies.

3

A pirate ship is fast approaching. What do you do?

A Hide below deck.

B Sail off in your own ship before they reach you.

C Bury your treasure and polish your sword.

4 Which of these animals would you choose as a pet?

A Cute rabbit.

B Ship's cat.

C Talking parrot.

5 What do you like to wear on your head?

A A baseball cap.

B A bandana.

C A tricorn hat, of course.

6 What are your hobbies?

A Reading and playing the piano.

B Cooking and dancing.

C Swordfighting and finding treasure.

YOUR SCORE!

Check your answers, then see what your score rating is below!

Mostly As You're more of a landlubber than a buccaneer. Stick to dry land.

Mostly Bs You might like life on the ocean waves. Why not try becoming a pirate?

Mostly Cs You're perfect pirate material and would make a fearsome captain for any ship!

Crazy crew

Draw the right expression for each
Pirate in this motley crew.

Petrified pirates

Connect the dots to find out why these pirates are so scared.

1
28
2
27
3
26
4
8
7
9
5
13   11
10 6
14
12
25   15
16
19
24 17
18   21   20
22
23

Answer is at the back of the book.

Pirate memory game

Look at the things that Pirate Pete is thinking about for one minute.

Then turn the page and draw everything you can remember.

On behalf of the swashbuckling League of Pirates,

I hereby declare that:

....

is an

Honorary Pirate

and very able crew member!

By order of:

....

17

28
B3 = Shark
F1 = Island
A5 = Volcano
E3 = Ship
H8 = Booty

32
1 c – map-reading
2 a – sailing the seven seas
3 b – hobbling on one leg
4 e – stowing away
5 f – sword-fighting
6 d – finding treasure

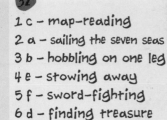 ANSWERS

36

50

56

49

61

66 The odd one out is f.

68

59
1. Ahoy
2. Booty
3. Splice the mainbrace

60
1. Ship
2. Castle
3. Sea Monster

69 Pirate Moneybags is: Pete

74

84 a and e are a pair

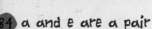

87

92